JAZZ EXERCISES, MINUETS, ETUDES & PIECES FOR PIANO

2ND EDITION

BY OSCAR PETERSON

cover photo: © Herman Leonard Photography, LLC

ISBN 978-0-634-09979-3

HAL•LEONARD®
CORPORATION

7777 W. BLUEMOUND RD. P.O. BOX 13819 MILWAUKEE, WI 53213

In Australia Contact:
Hal Leonard Australia Pty. Ltd.
4 Lentara Court
Cheltenham, Victoria, 3192 Australia
Email: ausadmin@halleonard.com

Visit Hal Leonard Online at
www.halleonard.com

PREFACE

Jazz piano can be a very enjoyable musical experience from a listening standpoint, to everyone, both adult and youngster alike. However, when a person, whether studied or not classically speaking, attempts to enter the jazz world from a playing aspect, he often finds himself hamstrung by many varied musical inadequacies. Very few people truly ever attribute their lack of ability to the proper cause, I feel. Many of them blame what they term their creative inability to conceive jazz phrases, without stopping to realize that a jazz technique in many ways is a completely new form of technique when compared with the classical. It is with this primary aspect in mind that I have conceived this set of beginner's exercises. I feel that if the player honestly and sincerely learns the jazz exercises one at a time, and after having completed one, then applies that learning to the little jazz minuet that matches the exercise, he will be, in effect, conditioning the hands for proceeding into deeper jazz playing.

It is vitally important that all fingering given in both hands be followed completely. In the exercises where no fingering is given in one hand, I feel that the player should instinctively have no trouble finding the proper digital position to give the greatest ease of hand movement, thereby achieving a better tonal result on the piano.

I hope that this book of jazz exercises, minuets, etudes, and pieces opens a new world of pianistic command to the avid young pianist.

Oscar Peterson

CONTENTS

BIOGRAPHY

Oscar Peterson was born August 15, 1925 in Montreal, Quebec, Canada. His parents were immigrants from the British West Indies and the Virgin Islands. His father, Daniel Peterson, was boatswain on a sailing vessel when he met Olivia John in Montreal, where she worked as a cook and housekeeper for an English family. They decided to remain in Canada, get married, and start a family.

Oscar was the fourth of five children. Originally taking an interest in the trumpet, a childhood bout of tuberculosis switched Oscar's emphasis to the piano under the tutelage of his father and later his sister, Daisy. His musical talent soon surpassed the capabilities of home teaching, and he was sent outside of the home to study. Oscar studied with the gifted Hungarian classical pianist Paul de Marky, and a warm and respectful musical friendship developed between the two.

In 1947, Oscar formed his first Canadian trio and retained this format of performance for the next several years. During this time, he remained dedicated to establishing a true trio sound. At an appearance in the Alberta Lounge in 1949, impresario Norman Granz heard him and enticed him into making a guest appearance at Carnegie Hall with his all-star concert troupe known as "Jazz at the Philharmonic." Leaving the audience awestruck, Oscar returned home for a year, then rejoined JATP as a steady member in 1950. He commenced recording with Norman Granz's Mercury label, and formed his first American duo with bassist Ray Brown.

In 1950, he was awarded the *DownBeat* Award for Best Jazz Pianist. He would go on to garner this award twelve more times during his career. He continued his extensive touring of the United States, and later, as a musical ambassador for the Canadian government, he toured Europe, Africa, South America, the Far East, and even Russia.

During these busy touring schedules, he formed a jazz school in Toronto, known as the Advanced School of Contemporary Music, which attracted students from all over the world. While on tour, he would conduct seminars and, amazingly, found time to compose his "Canadiana Suite," a salute to Canada, which was recorded with his trio and released worldwide.

Oscar has recorded with many of the jazz greats over the years. His varied albums with these giants include recordings with Louis Armstrong, Ella Fitzgerald, Count Basie, Duke Ellington, Dizzy Gillespie, Roy Eldridge, Coleman Hawkins, and Charlie Parker, but it has been the recordings with his various trios that have brought him recognition from numerous places around the world.

In recent years, Oscar has been devoting more and more time to composition. His "Hymn to Freedom" became one of the crusade hymns during the civil rights movement in the United States. He has composed music for motion pictures, including the Canadian film *Big North* for Ontario Place in Toronto, as well as the

BIOGRAPHY

thriller *Silent Partner*, for which he won a Genie Award in 1978. His collaboration with Norman McLaren, titled *Begone Dull Care*, won awards all over the world. Oscar also composed the soundtrack for the film *Fields of Endless Day*, which traced the Underground Railroad used by African-Americans escaping to Canada during the slavery era. In addition, he has worked with the National Film Board of Canada.

Oscar followed his motion picture work with a ballet commissioned by Les Ballets Jazz du Canada, which included a special waltz for the city of Toronto titled "City Lights." Other compositional projects included "A Suite Called Africa" and a salute to Johann Sebastian Bach's 300th birthday, written for trio and orchestra. These were followed by the "Easter Suite," which was commissioned by the BBC of London and performed with a trio on Good Friday, 1984, via nationwide television. This particular production is still broadcast annually. He also composed music for the opening ceremonies of the 1988 Calgary Winter Olympic Games. In addition to all of these, Oscar has composed over 300 other tunes, most of which have been published.

Oscar has appeared on a wide array of television productions, and has hosted his own specials where he interviewed and played with a variety of guests. His widespread appeal gave way to an unusual range in personalities that included Anthony Burgess, Andrew Lloyd Webber, Tim Rice, and Edward Heath, the former Prime Minister of England.

Oscar prefers not to use his celebrity to sway political opinions, yet he remains dedicated to the belief that his native Canada has a responsibility in leading the world in equality and justice. With this in mind, he has taken a firm stand to promote recognition and fair treatment for Canada's multi-cultural community. Because of his efforts in this field, Mr. Peterson was inducted as an Officer of the Order of Canada in 1972. He was promoted to Companion of the Order, Canada's highest civilian honor, in 1984.

In 1993, Oscar was awarded the Glenn Gould Prize. He was the third recipient of the Prize, the first with a unanimous decision, and the first ever from the realm of jazz. Over the years, Mr. Peterson has been awarded many honorary degrees, and a host of other awards, including the Praemium Imperiale (the Arts equivalent of the Nobel Prize), the UNESCO International Music Prize, the Queen's Medal, the Toronto Arts Award for Lifetime Achievement, the Governor General's Performing Arts Award, and most recently the President's Award from the International Association for Jazz Education.

Despite a mild stroke in 1993, which at first debilitated his left hand, Oscar recovered to continue his yearly pattern of worldwide concert tours, recordings, and composition.

Mr. Peterson resides in the quiet city of Mississauga, Ontario. As a citizen he insists on his privacy, which he jealously guards. His hobbies include fishing, photography and astronomy, and he is an avid audiophile and synthesist. His home contains his own private recording studio, where he can work but still be able to enjoy his family life. His passion for life, love, and music is stronger than ever.

EXERCISE No.1

EXERCISE 1 AND MINUET 1

Exercise one attempts to give the player two things. First, strength. The player moves from the middle of the right hand to the last finger of the right hand, then moves from the thumb of the right hand to the middle of the hand. Secondly, if practised properly, the player should be able to achieve better digital control on this type of phrasing without rocking the hand from side to side.

MINUET No.1

EXERCISE 2 AND MINUET 2

This exercise and minuet are merely to induce in the player the ability to phrase jazz-wise in his left hand when called upon to do so. Here also he should strive for a completely even tonal result.

EXERCISE No. 2

MINUET No. 2

8

EXERCISE 3 AND MINUET 3

This exercise and minuet deals primarily with what I feel are the two weakest fingers of the jazz pianist's right hand (the fourth and fifth fingers). On playing this exercise and piece the player should attempt to keep the listener (or his instructor) from knowing that he is using his fifth finger on his right hand. Usually this is a pitfall in jazz playing. The student will notice that the fifth finger is employed in the middle of the phrase rather than at the end which is the usual jazz custom.

EXERCISE No. 3

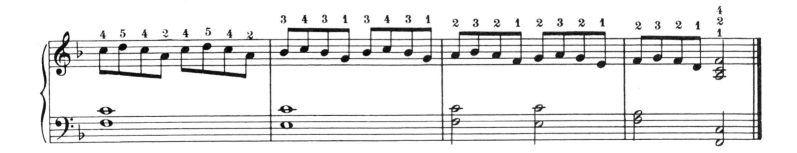

MINUET No. 3

EXERCISE No.4

EXERCISE 4 AND MINUET 4

This exercise and piece are merely to give the beginner the chance to formulate in his own mind the format and content of the blues from a background standpoint. Very elementary harmonic movement is employed and after both exercise and minuet have been learned thoroughly, the player should attempt to improvise his own right hand lines on the background given here.

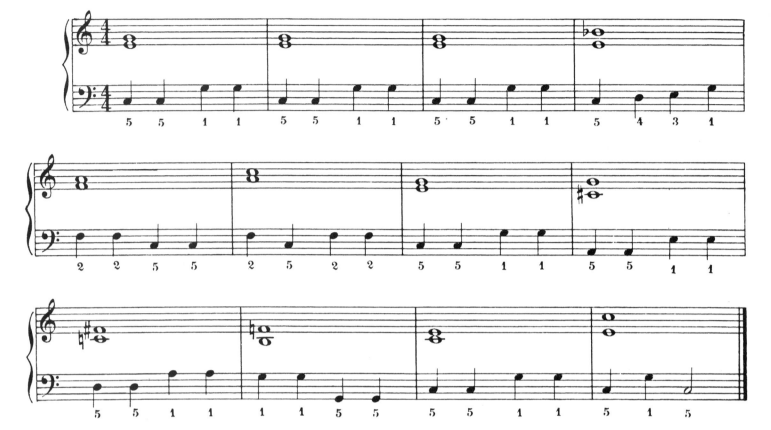

MINUET No.4

EXERCISE 5 AND MINUET 5

We now approach the walking bass line. I feel now that with the movement employed the player should gain a much firmer understanding of what a bass player does for the pianist on the blues in the primary stage. Again I state that after command is gained of these two pieces, the player should attempt to conceive lines on this given bass.

EXERCISE No.5

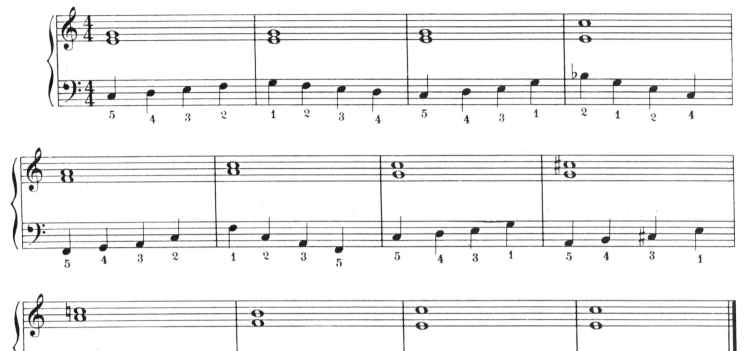

MINUET No.5

EXERCISE No.6

The left hand pattern now enters the form of boogie woogie. This is a very important exercise and should be thoroughly learned before any other lines are attempted against the left hand. Incidentally this should represent a great challenge from this aspect because it is fairly difficult to move the right hand line to any depth against a bass line that is quite busy such as the one provided.

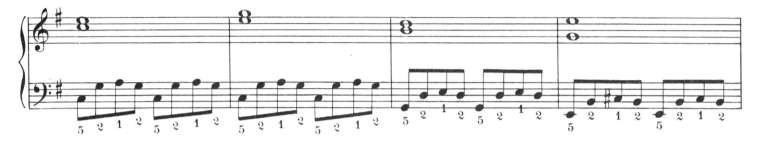

MINUET No.6

EXERCISE 7 AND MINUET 7

We now employ the stop and go bass figures. This gives us the ability to change from an elementary sense of rhythmic pattern in the left hand, introducing from time to time a straight four as a form of relief. The melody in the jazz minuet should be played in a very legato manner in order to give the listener a sense of cohesiveness between the two hands.

EXERCISE No.7

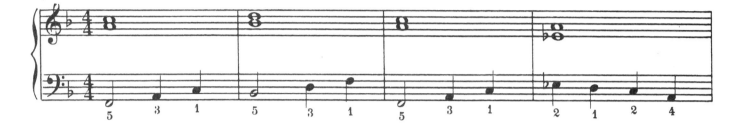

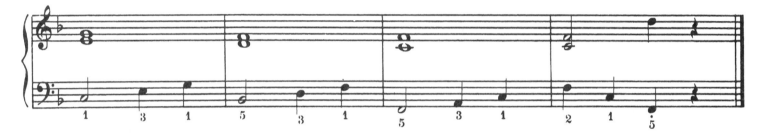

MINUET No.7

14

EXERCISE No. 8

EXERCISE 8 AND MINUET 8

Here we employ a steady walking bass figure in the exercise. In the minuet we employ fairly busy lines. The player should attempt different types of articulation in order to obtain the final and correct jazz feeling that he desires. In doing this he should then be able to realize how the jazz player (professional) changes the complete complexion of a tune by changing his articulation.

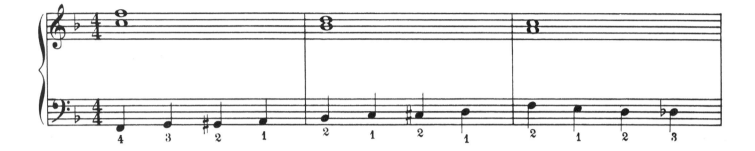

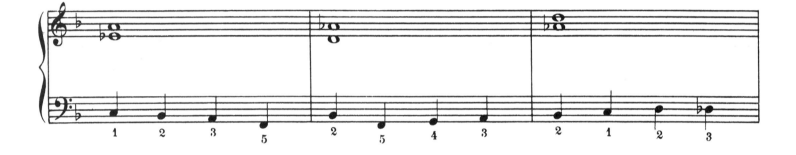

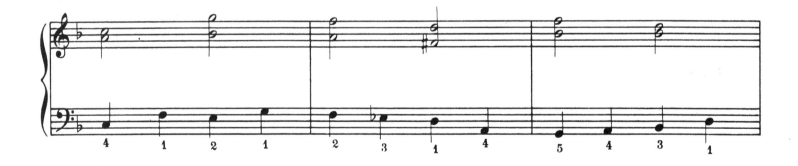

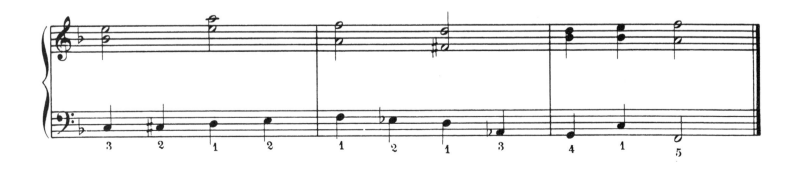

MINUET No.8

EXERCISE 9 AND MINUET 9

This is an exercise in double hands in which once again the player has a choice of articulation. However, the fingering should be studied carefully so that he realizes that in order to articulate with complete ease, his hands must be free of any keyboard entanglements.

EXERCISE No. 9

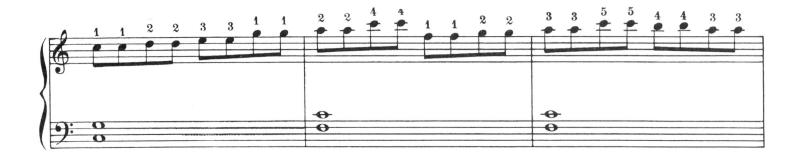

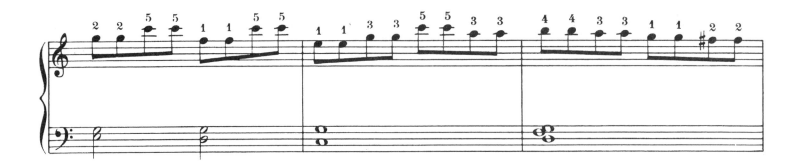

MINUET No.9

EXERCISE No.10

EXERCISE 10 AND MINUET 10

Exercise ten is vitally important for here we have the walking bass line in eighth notes. Later on in the minuet, we add a line of eighth notes in the right hand also. The trick here is to keep the primary sense of rhythmic impetus in the left hand while playing the right hand lines with an even legato feel.

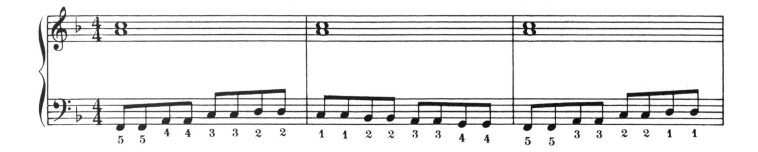

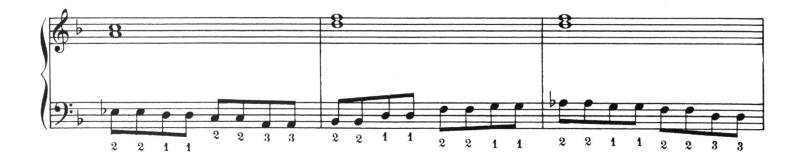

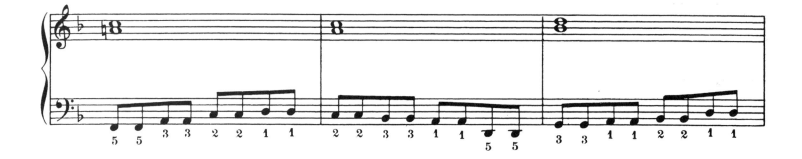

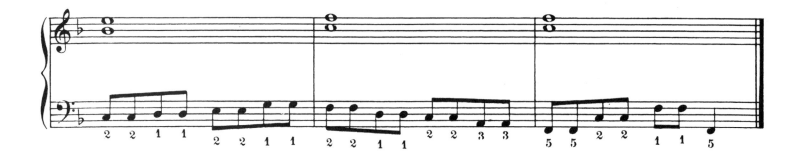

MINUET No.10

EXERCISE 11 AND MINUET 11

Many jazz pianists including yours truly at various times employ a double melodic line using two hands. Many times this is used to give a deeper rhythmic projection to the melodic line. At other times it is used in a very free-flight manner (primarily during fast tempos). Another aspect of the ability to play double lines is that it can be very effective when the pianist is doubling the same line as another instrumentalist. You will notice in the minuet that both hands at various times get a chance to play background and lead. This is an exercise that should be practiced carefully in order to give the pianist the ability to make this change as smoothly as possible.

EXERCISE No.11

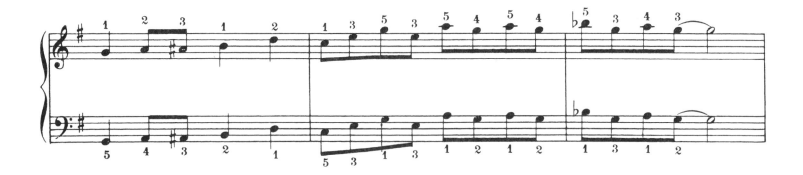

MINUET No.11

EXERCISE 12 AND MINUET 12

We deal now with the aspect of a moving line and chords in both hands. The minuet bears a very close resemblance to the exercise here, so the transition from the exercise to the piece should be very easy. It is important to give each underlying harmony its proper rhythmic value and tonal respect.

EXERCISE No.12

MINUET No.12

EXERCISE 13 AND MINUET 13

In exercise thirteen we prepare for changing rhythms in both hands. Upon reaching the minuet, if any difficulty is experienced, the player should leave the minuet and return to the exercise, for the secret lies in first imprinting the depth of the melodic line in either hand. If any other trouble is encountered here, the player should return to exercise and minuet number eleven.

EXERCISE No. 13

MINUET No. 13

24

Exercise fourteen should be practiced until the player achieves a fleet but confirmed sense of interpretation. When this has been accomplished, he should then apply this technique to the minuet.

EXERCISE No. 14

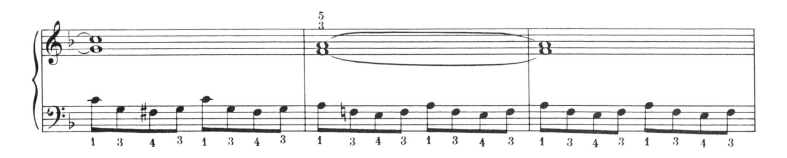

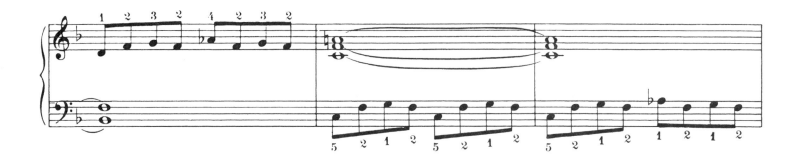

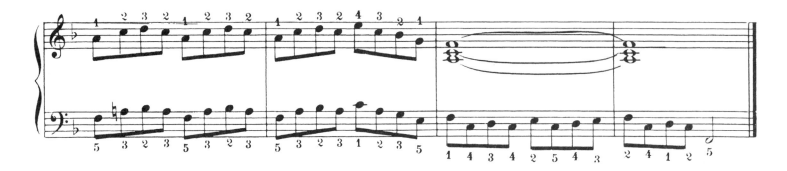

MINUET No. 14

ETUDE No.1

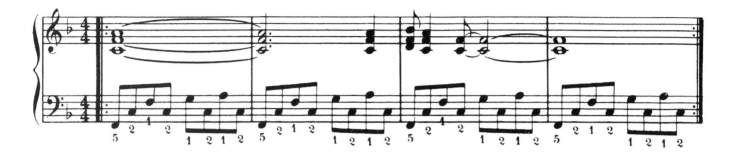

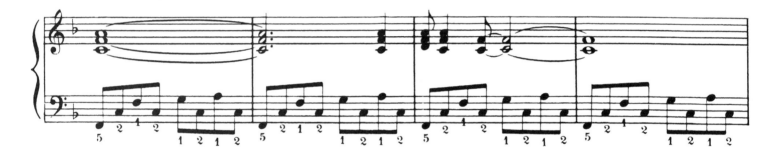

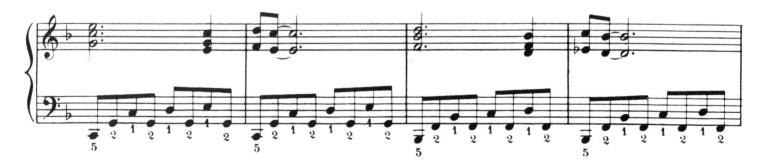

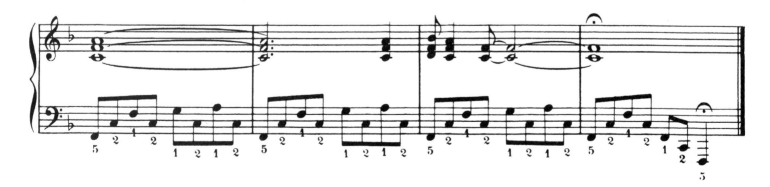

PIECE No.1

ETUDE No.2

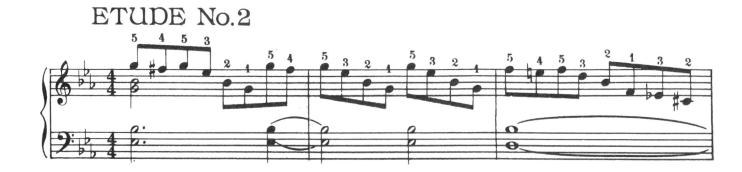

PIECE No.2

30

ETUDE No.3

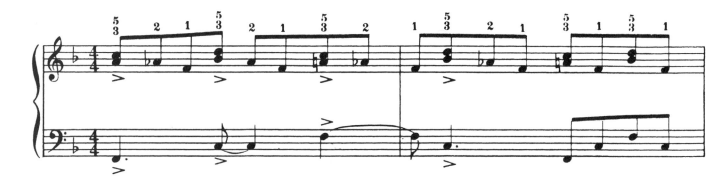

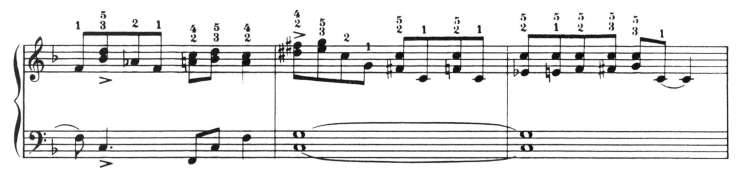

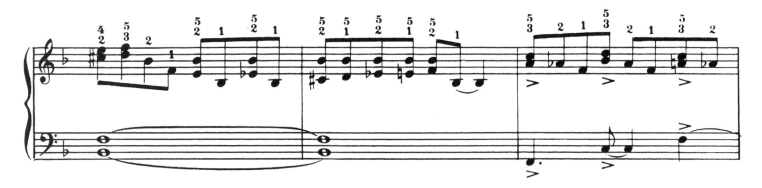

PIECE No.3

ETUDE No. 4

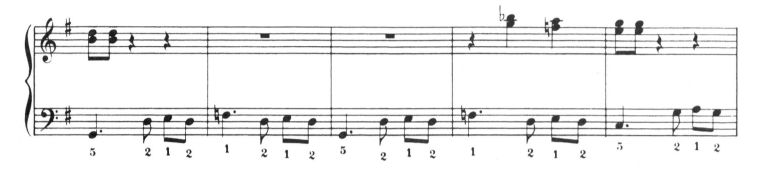

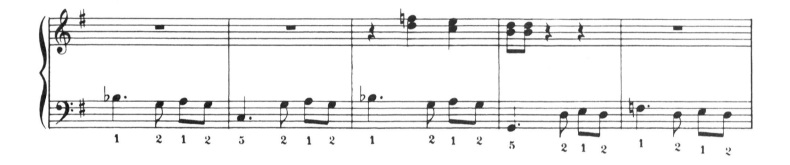

PIECE No. 4

ETUDE No.5

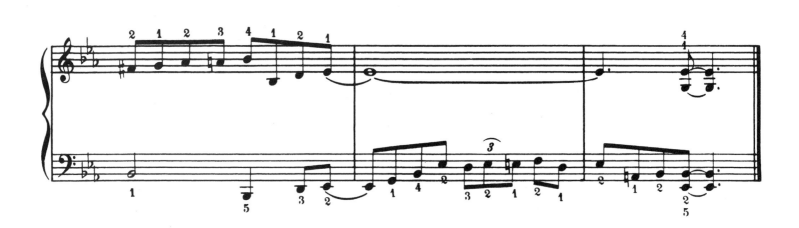

PIECE No.5

ETUDE No.6

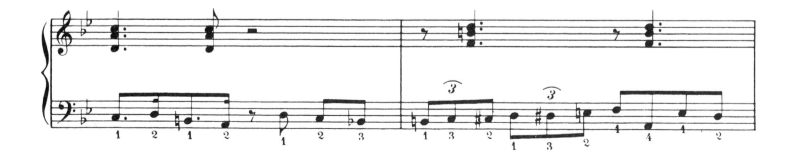

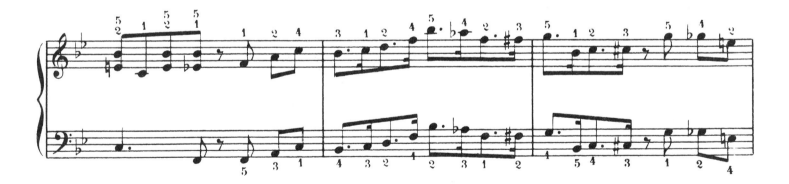

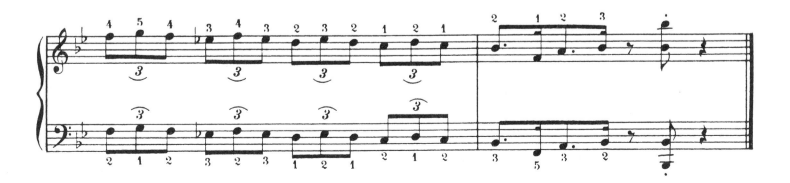

PIECE No.6

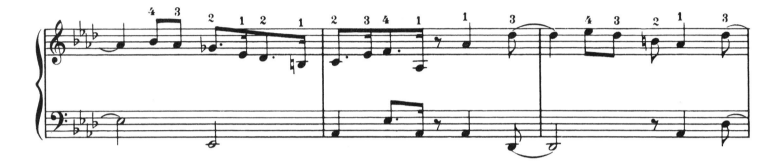

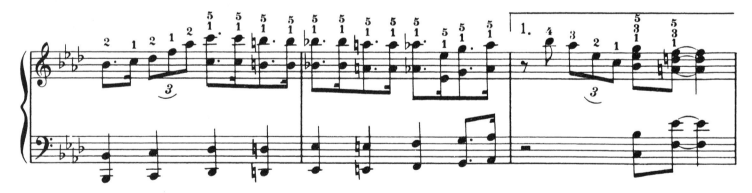

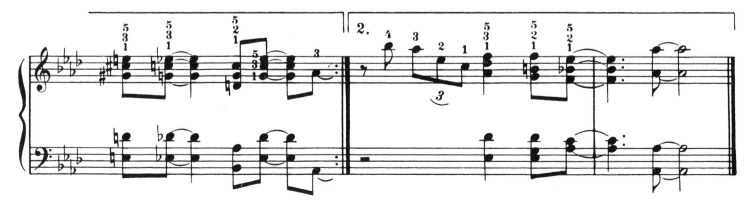

ETUDE No.7

PIECE No.7

ETUDE No. 8

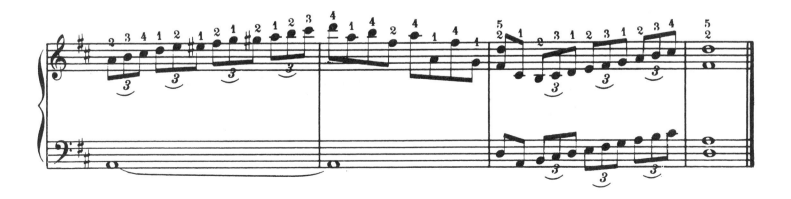

PIECE No.8

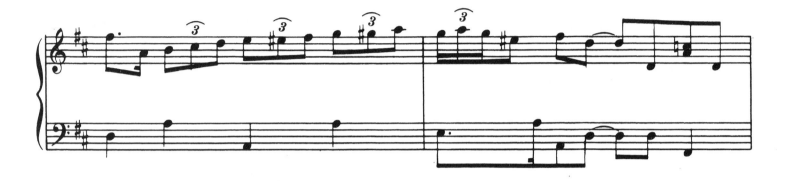

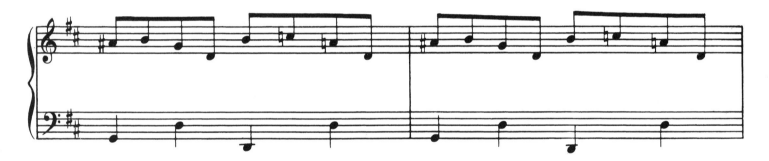

PIECE No.9

ETUDE No.10

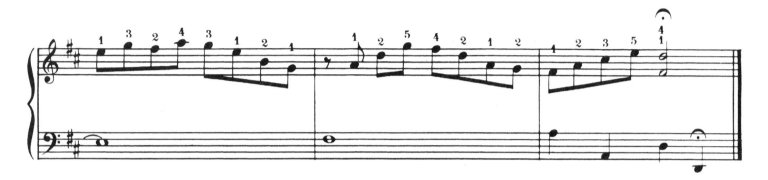

PIECE No.10

EXERCISE No.1

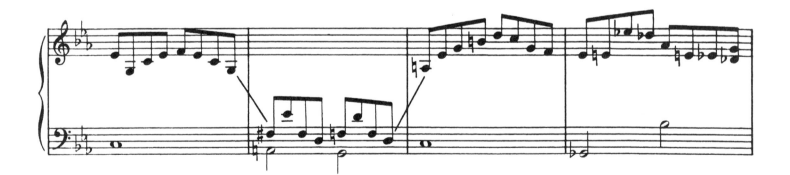

EXERCISE No.2

EXERCISE No. 3

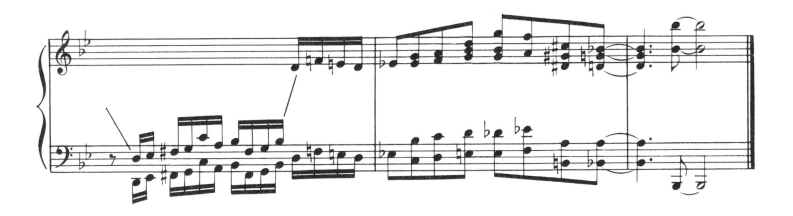

EXERCISE No.4

EXERCISE No.5

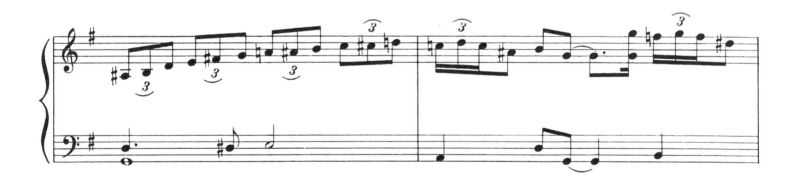

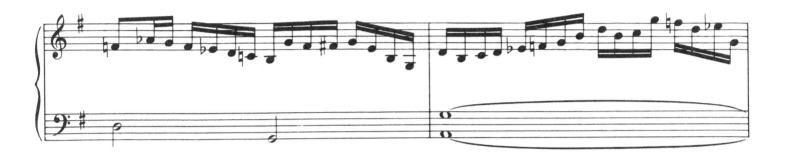

EXERCISE No.6

EXERCISE No.7

EXERCISE No. 8

EXERCISE No.9

EXERCISE No.10

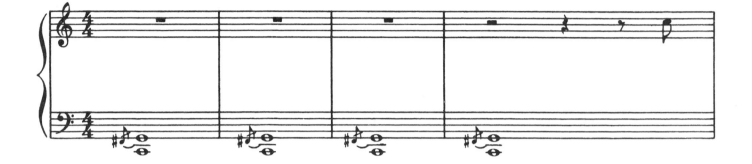

EXERCISE No.11

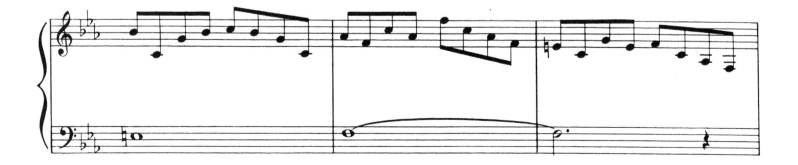

EXERCISE No.12

EXERCISE No.13

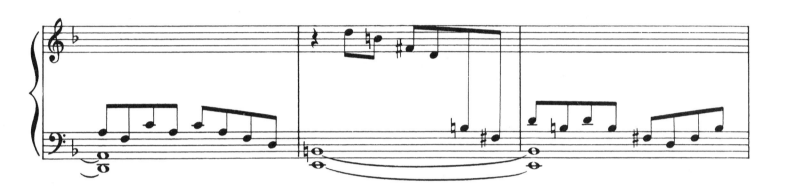

Hal Leonard Presents More Publications Featuring
OSCAR PETERSON

OSCAR PETERSON – CLASSIC TRIO PERFORMANCES

Signature Licks Series for Piano
14 trademark pieces: C-Jam Blues • Cheek to Cheek • Come Rain or Come Shine • Do Nothin' Till You Hear from Me • Don't Get Around Much Anymore • The Girl from Ipanema • I Got It Bad and That Ain't Good • Indiana • The Lady Is a Tramp • Lover • My One and Only Love • Quiet Nights of Quiet Stars • Take the "A" Train • That Old Black Magic.
00695871 Book/CD Pack $22.99

OSCAR PETERSON – JAZZ EXERCISES, MINUETS, ETUDES & PIECES FOR PIANO

In this book, Oscar Peterson offers dozens of pieces designed to empower the student, whether novice or classically trained, with the technique needed to become an accomplished jazz pianist.
00311225 ....$14.99

OSCAR PETERSON – JAZZ PIANO SOLOS

8 Peterson classics: The Continental • Gravy Waltz • Hallelujah Time • Hymn to Freedom • Roundalay • Blues for Smedley • The Smudge • The Strut.
00672542 ....$19.99

OSCAR PETERSON – A JAZZ PORTRAIT OF FRANK SINATRA

12 Sinatra standards: All of Me • The Birth of the Blues • Come Dance with Me • How About You? • I Get a Kick Out of You • It Happened in Monterey • Just in Time • Learnin' the Blues • Saturday Night (Is the Loneliest Night of the Week) • (Love Is) The Tender Trap • Witchcraft • You Make Me Feel So Young.
00672562 Artist Transcriptions for Piano..........$19.95

OSCAR PETERSON – NIGHT TRAIN

11 note-for-note transcriptions: Bags' Groove • Band Call • C-Jam Blues • Easy Does It • Georgia on My Mind • The Honeydripper • Hymn to Freedom • I Got It Bad and That Ain't Good • Moten Swing • Night Train • Things Ain't What They Used to Be.
00264094 Artist Transcriptions for Piano..........$19.99

OSCAR PETERSON – OMNIBOOK

Nearly 40 full transcriptions: All of Me • Between the Devil and the Deep Blue Sea • Falling in Love with Love • Georgia on My Mind • I Got It Bad and That Ain't Good • If I Were a Bell • In the Wee Small Hours of the Morning • Love Is Here to Stay • On Green Dolphin Street • Sometimes I'm Happy • The Song Is You • Tangerine • That Old Black Magic • Whisper Not • You Stepped Out of a Dream • Yours Is My Heart Alone • and more.
00139880 Piano Transcriptions $39.99
00148435 C Instruments $24.99
00148436 B-Flat Instruments.............................$24.99
00148437 E-Flat Instruments.............................$24.99
00148438 Bass Clef Instruments........................$24.99

OSCAR PETERSON – ORIGINALS

Transcriptions, lead sheets and performance notes for 5 original Peterson compositions: Cakewalk • The Gentle Waltz • He Has Gone • Love Ballade • Sushi. Includes a bio and preface.
00672544 ....$14.99

OSCAR PETERSON PLAYS DUKE ELLINGTON

17 transcriptions: Band Call • C-Jam Blues • Caravan • Cotton Tail • Do Nothin' Till You Hear from Me • Don't Get Around Much Anymore • I Got It Bad and That Ain't Good • In a Mellow Tone • John Hardy's Wife • Just a Settin' and a Rockin' • Night Train • Prelude to a Kiss • Rockin' in Rhythm • Satin Doll • Sophisticated Lady • Take the "A" Train • Things Ain't What They Used to Be.
00672531 Artist Transcriptions for Piano..........$24.99

OSCAR PETERSON PLAYS STANDARDS

Signature Licks Series for Piano
Study and play these enduring jazz standards: All of Me • Between the Devil and the Deep Blue Sea • Falling in Love with Love • Fly Me to the Moon • Georgia on My Mind • I Love You • In a Mellow Tone • It's All Right with Me • It's Only a Paper Moon • My Heart Stood Still • On the Sunny Side of the Street • When Lights Are Low.
00695900 Book/Online Audio $24.99

OSCAR PETERSON – A ROYAL WEDDING SUITE

Includes: Heraldry • It's On • Jubilation • Lady Di's Waltz • Let the World Sing • London Gets Ready • Royal Honeymoon • When Summer Comes.
00672563 Artist Transcriptions for Piano..........$19.99

OSCAR PETERSON – TRACKS

Includes 10 tunes: Basin Street Blues • A Child Is Born • Dancing on the Ceiling • Django • Give Me the Simple Life • Honeysuckle Rose • If I Should Lose You • Ja-Da • Just a Gigolo • A Little Jazz Exercise.
00672569 Artist Transcriptions for Piano..........$19.99

THE VERY BEST OF OSCAR PETERSON

18 songs: A Child Is Born • The Continental • The Girl from Ipanema • Gravy Waltz • I'm Old Fashioned • It Ain't Necessarily So • Little Girl Blue • Love Is Here to Stay • Moanin' • My One and Only Love • Noreen's Nocturne • On the Trail • Over the Rainbow • Place St. Henri • Rockin' Chair • 'Round Midnight • Stella by Starlight • Sweet Georgia Brown.
00672534 Artist Transcriptions for Piano..........$22.95

THE OSCAR PETERSON TRIO – CANADIANA SUITE

Eight songs: Ballad to the East • Blues of the Prairies • Hogtown Blues • Land of the Misty Giants • Laurentide Waltz • March Past • Place St. Henri • Wheatland.
00672543 Piano Transcriptions $15.99

OSCAR PETERSON TRIOS

19 authentic transcriptions, including: Blues Etude • Hymn to Freedom • Misty • Quiet Nights of Quiet Stars • Witchcraft • and more.
00672533 Artist Transcriptions for Piano..........$29.99

HAL•LEONARD®

View songlists and order today from your favorite music retailer at **halleonard.com**

0521
079